THE
EASTER
STORY

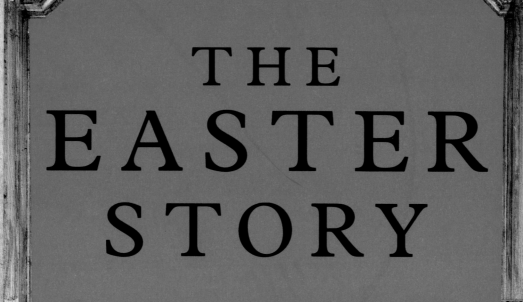

THE
EASTER
STORY

BRIAN WILDSMITH

ALFRED A. KNOPF
New York

Once, a long time ago, a little donkey was brought to Jesus. The little donkey had never been ridden before, but Jesus spoke gently to him, and soon he stopped being afraid.

Jesus climbed onto the donkey's back, and they set off for Jerusalem.

As Jesus and his friends drew near the city, there were great crowds standing along the road. The little donkey was amazed to see so many people. Some had spread their clothes on the road. Branches cut down from the palm trees were spread there too, all for him to walk on.

"Hosanna!" the people shouted. "Hosanna! It's the man who comes from God."

By the time they reached Jerusalem, the crowds had grown more excited. Some people asked, ''Who's that, sitting on the back of the donkey?'' Others replied, ''It is the prophet Jesus from Nazareth in Galilee.''

The little donkey lifted his head proudly as they entered the city.

The little donkey carried Jesus through the streets until they stopped in front of the Temple. People came from all around to pray there. Jesus went inside and saw that it was like a market, full of people buying and selling.

Angrily, he drove them all out, shouting, "It is written, 'My house shall be a house of prayer,' not a den of thieves!"

Then every day that week, he taught and healed people in the Temple.

The donkey stayed with Jesus in the city. Thursday was a holiday, and on that night they walked through the streets to a small house. Jesus went inside to have supper with his friends. Through the window the little donkey saw Jesus breaking the bread.

"Take and eat this," said Jesus, holding the bread. "It is my
body." And the donkey watched as Jesus lifted up a cup of wine.
"Take and drink this," Jesus said. "It is my blood."

After supper, the little donkey followed Jesus and his friends to the garden of Gethsemane. Jesus said to them, "Sit here and keep watch while I pray." The donkey sat and waited, but everyone else fell asleep.

Suddenly a crowd of people came into the garden. They were led by Judas, one of Jesus' friends, and they seized Jesus and dragged him away. Judas had betrayed his friend.

The rest of Jesus' friends ran away. The little donkey and Simon Peter didn't run away but followed the crowd through the city. Three times Simon Peter was stopped. "You are a friend of Jesus," people said.

Simon Peter was afraid. "No," he said. "Not I."

At last they came to the house of Caiaphas, the High Priest of the Temple.
The donkey heard Caiaphas ask Jesus, "Are you the Son of God?"
  "I am," Jesus replied.

The High Priest said, "You have heard these terrible words. How can any man speak this way of God? What do you say?"

"He deserves to die," everyone cried.

The crowd left Caiaphas's house and took Jesus to Pilate, the Roman governor, to see that he was punished.

The little donkey watched as Jesus stood in front of Pilate, the chief priests from the Temple, and a huge crowd of people.

"Are you the King of the Jews?" asked Pilate.

"Those are your words," said Jesus.

The priests then accused Jesus of many things. "Have you no answer to make to them?" asked Pilate. But Jesus didn't answer.

"What shall I do with him?" Pilate asked the crowd.

"Crucify him," everyone shouted.

"Take him and crucify him, then," said Pilate. "I wash my hands of him."

So the soldiers took Jesus away. They put a crown made of thorns on his head and made fun of him. "Hail, King of the Jews!" they said. They gave him a huge cross of wood and forced him to carry it.

"If only I could help him," thought the donkey sadly. But a man came out of the crowd and helped Jesus to carry his cross.

The little donkey followed as they led Jesus to a hill outside the city.

There they crucified him between two thieves.

Late that night, a rich man named Joseph asked Pilate for the body of Jesus. He wrapped the body in a clean linen sheet. It was too heavy for him to carry.

Joseph placed the body of Jesus on the donkey's back, and the little donkey carried it to a new tomb, which had been cut out of a rock. Joseph laid the body inside and rolled a huge stone in front of the entrance.

Early Sunday morning, Mary, the mother of Jesus, and Mary Magdalene came to the tomb. But when they got there, they found that the stone had been rolled away and the body of Jesus was gone.

The donkey saw two angels where Jesus' body had been. "He is not here,"
the angels said. "He is alive again."

Mary and Mary Magdalene left the tomb, and the donkey followed until they came to a garden. A man was standing there. It was Jesus.

The women were frightened, but Jesus said to them, "Don't be afraid. Run
and tell my friends to go up to Galilee, and they will see me there."

Jesus' friends were so happy to see him again. He stayed with them for forty days, teaching them about the Kingdom of God. But Jesus knew that it was near the time for him to leave this earth.

One morning, he went up to his father in Heaven.

The next day, one of Jesus' friends took the little donkey back to his home. And the donkey stayed there for the rest of his life, remembering the kind and good man he had carried on his back to Jerusalem.

FOR MAUREEN VERONICA

Gracious thanks to Mira Avrech, Abraham Rosenthal, and the Israel Tourist Board for their great kindness and
generosity in the preparation of this book.

This is a Borzoi Book published by Alfred A. Knopf, Inc.

Manufactured in Hong Kong 10 9 8 7 6 5 4 3 2

Library of Congress Cataloging-in-Publication Data
Wildsmith, Brian   An Easter story / by Brian Wildsmith   p.   cm.   Summary: The story of the last days of
Jesus' life, the crucifixion, and the resurrection, as seen through the eyes of a small donkey.
ISBN 0-679-84727-8   (trade)
1. Jesus Christ—Resurrection—Juvenile literature. 2. Jesus Christ—Passion—Juvenile literature. 3. Bible
stories, English—N.T. Gospels. [1. Jesus Christ—Resurrection. 2. Jesus Christ—Passion. 3. Bible stories—
N.T.] I. Title BT481.W54 1994 232.96—dc20 93-25097